BEFORE
THEY WERE
AUTHORS

BEFORE THEY WERE AUTHORS

Famous Writers as Kids

Elizabeth Haidle

HOUGHTON MIFFLIN HARCOURT
Boston   New York

hmhco.com

The illustrations in this book were rendered
in watercolor, ink, and digital.
The text type was set in Eke.
The display type was set in Kikster.

ISBN: 978-1-328-80153-1

Manufactured in China
SCP 10 9 8 7 6 5 4 3 2 1
4500749677

*To my earliest favorite book—Miss Suzy,
by Miriam Young and illustrated by Arnold Lobel—
about a displaced squirrel who makes her home
wherever she goes.*

WHAT MAKES A WRITER?

Many of us wonder about the stories behind the stories of best-selling authors . . .

Were their bookshelves stocked with the very best books? Did they read Shakespeare while listening to Mozart? Was there something magical in their after-school snacks?

As it turns out, each of these authors followed a different route. A few started writing as soon as they could hold a pencil. Others began later, only after failing at other jobs. Some writers invented invisible worlds, while others transformed the mundane details of their own lives.

Sometimes, words on paper helped them to cope with the difficulties of life: illness, loneliness, transferring schools, or the death of a loved one. Many discovered the joy of collaborating—acting out stories with friends or selling homemade comics at school.

A few threads of similarity are woven throughout these authors' lives: A love of reading—if their house wasn't already crammed with books, the library became another home.

Writing and rewriting played a key role, though not always in the form of stories. Several authors wrote letters or kept personal diaries. Some wrote privately, in a secret code.

Determination was crucial, as the road to fame was never smooth. Encouragement from a mentor or teacher often made the difference when it came to braving the toughest years. Most authors endured rejections. Some got their books published only to have them banned. More often than not, day jobs paid bills while writing was squeezed into early mornings and late nights.

Pablo Picasso once commented on the universality of the creative impulse,

"EVERY CHILD IS AN ARTIST. THE PROBLEM IS HOW TO REMAIN ONE ONCE HE GROWS UP."

It's good to remember—all famous authors were once ordinary kids who felt that the writing of tales was something they couldn't live without.

CONTENTS

"THEN AWAY OUT IN THE WOODS I HEARD THAT KIND OF SOUND THAT A GHOST MAKES WHEN IT WANTS TO TELL ABOUT SOMETHING THAT'S ON ITS MIND AND CAN'T MAKE ITSELF UNDERSTOOD, AND SO CAN'T REST EASY IN ITS GRAVE, AND HAS TO GO ABOUT THAT WAY EVERY NIGHT, GRIEVING. I GOT SO DOWN-HEARTED AND SCARED I DID WISH I HAD SOME COMPANY."

— *The Adventures of Huckleberry Finn*

MARK TWAIN

1835
Born in Florida, Missouri

1872
Publishes *Roughing It*

1876
Publishes *The Adventures of Tom Sawyer*

1880
Publishes *A Tramp Abroad*

1884
Publishes *The Adventures of Huckleberry Finn*

1910
Dies in Redding, Connecticut

Mark Twain was born as Halley's Comet blazed through the night sky, and he died the day the comet returned, 75 years later. Named Samuel Clemens and later known by the pen name of Mark Twain, he would become America's first celebrity author . . . after many failed attempts at other jobs.

When he was four, young Samuel's family moved to a small Southern town on the Mississippi River.

The landscape and people of the region made such an imprint on him that his most famous tales would be set there.

Sam's specialty was trouble, right from the start. Sickly during his early years, the boy constantly worried his parents. When his health improved, he caused distress of another kind. Skipping school in search of the best swimming hole, he nearly drowned on nine occasions. Any kind of mischief was cause for fun—from getting lost in caves to playing pranks at church.

Not everything about small-town life was idyllic for a boy like Sam . . .

Missouri was a slave state, and many of the cruelties Sam witnessed would become fuel for his justice-themed stories. Once, while fishing, Sam discovered the drowned body of a runaway slave.

When Sam's father died of pneumonia, debts forced the family to take in boarders and sell the furniture. Sam and his brothers had to find jobs. Their childhood had come to an abrupt end.

At age 12, Sam moved into the home of a printer to become a typesetting apprentice.

He worked in exchange for room and board. The hours were long, but the task of fitting hundreds of words into printing trays sharpened his vocabulary.

By age 15, Sam had quit school to work full-time at his brother's newspaper. He played "guest editor" while his brother was out of town, writing exaggerated tales under fake names. Though his schooling days were over, he educated himself at the local library after work.

At 17, he left home to seek his fortune and see the world. Sam tried many jobs, often falling on hard luck: journalist, lumberman, steamboat captain, and political advocate. His two-week experience as a soldier inspired a brief memoir: *The Private History of a Campaign That Failed*.

Casting about for purpose and stability, he hatched various short-term schemes for another two decades.

An attempt to mine silver with his brother in the Nevada Territory went poorly and left Sam with empty pockets. But he ended up with something more valuable than silver: a chance run-in with a fellow miner—a gambler who would bet on anything, even a frog. Sam was inspired to write about it.

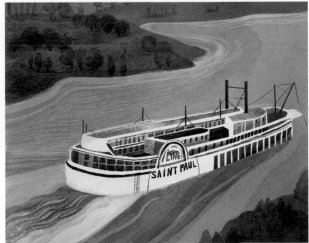

This happened to be the tale that jump-started his career. The story first appeared in the *New York Saturday Press* in 1865. Immensely popular, it was reprinted in newspapers across the nation. Sam eventually published it as an illustrated book.

Previously, Sam experimented with pen names such as W. Epaminondas Adrastus Perkins and Thomas Jefferson Snodgrass. He finally settled on Mark Twain—a riverboat term meaning "waters deep enough to pass through."

A streak of hilarious travel tales sparked Sam's international acclaim, earning him fans in many countries. Sam published books of his collected stories: *A Tramp Abroad* and *Roughing It*.

He promoted his writing on public lecture tours. Crowds flocked to hear the popular entertainer.

MARK TWAIN

LECTURE ON THE SANDWICH ISLANDS
DOORS OPEN AT 7 PM TROUBLE STARTS AT 8 PM

Sam decided to write his first novel for children. Inspired by his own boyhood in the South, *The Adventures of Tom Sawyer* was an immediate success, attracting readers of all ages.

He recast neighbors and family members as the heroes, villains, and bystanders. The river-town setting included Sam's favorite things: steamboats, caves, and fishing holes. Themes were drawn from his childhood memories of mischievous pranks, his love of nature, and his hatred of slavery.

The Adventures of Huckleberry Finn depicts the tale of a runaway slave from a child's point of view.

"[TOM] WAS IGNORANT, UNWASHED, INSUFFICIENTLY FED... BUT HE WAS THE ONLY REALLY INDEPENDENT PERSON...AND BY CONSEQUENCE HE WAS TRANQUILLY AND CONTINUOUSLY HAPPY AND WAS ENVIED BY THE REST OF US."

Sam's fame attracted important figures of his day, such as Nikola Tesla, the visionary inventor. The two met often in Tesla's laboratory.

Helen Keller—a blind, deaf, and mute author-activist—met Sam when she was a young girl. They became close friends and exchanged many letters.

On the topic of aging: "LIFE WOULD BE INFINITELY HAPPIER IF WE COULD ONLY BE BORN AT THE AGE OF EIGHTY AND GRADUALLY APPROACH EIGHTEEN."

Sam continued his lectures into old age, adding "public moralist" and "political philosopher" to his list of titles. When travel became impossible, Sam dictated his autobiography while lying in bed.

Sam had his last laugh from the grave. His mandate that the memoir be printed 100 years after his death made him the only author in history to publish bestsellers in three consecutive centuries.

Sam believed in writing with precision. He advised:

The difference between the almost right word and the right word is really a large matter—

it's the difference between the LIGHTNING BUG and the LIGHTNING.

"IF GROWING UP IS PAINFUL FOR THE SOUTHERN BLACK GIRL, BEING AWARE OF HER DISPLACEMENT IS THE RUST ON THE RAZOR THAT THREATENS THE THROAT."

— I Know Why the Caged Bird Sings

MAYA ANGELOU

1928
Born in St. Louis, Missouri

1969
Publishes autobiography *I Know Why the Caged Bird Sings*

1971
Publishes poetry collection *Just Give Me a Cool Drink of Water 'fore I Diiie*

1974–2013
Publishes six more memoirs, ending with *Mom & Me & Mom*

2014
Dies in Winston-Salem, North Carolina

When Maya Angelou was only three, her parents divorced. She was sent to another city with her brother. A tag on her wrist bore her birth name:

Living with her grandmother in the South took some getting used to. In grade school, her attempt to recite a poem at church involved stuttering the first lines, forgetting the end, racing out the door, and crying all the way home. The shy girl who was paralyzed by stage fright would eventually become a public performer.

Marguerite would reinvent herself over time. (At the onset of her stage career, she began to use her nickname from childhood, Maya.) As a young girl, she never imagined that she would someday find herself in jobs that required courage and confidence: working as a trolley conductor, a dancer, a singer, an actress, and a speaker.

As a child, Maya learned not just to survive, but to thrive. She took comfort in her favorite things:

FAVORITE PERSON: BROTHER

"Bailey was the greatest person in my world."

FAVORITE SNACK: PINEAPPLE

"My obsession with pineapples nearly drove me mad."

FAVORITE MUSIC: JAZZ

"I could crawl into the space between the notes and turn my back to loneliness."

At the age of seven, a terrible crisis occurred while she stayed with her mother in St. Louis. Maya quit speaking for five years.

Fortunately, there were strong women in her life. Vivian, her mother, was a fierce ally. Maya recalls her as . . .

Grandmother Henderson was a clever businesswoman who ran her own store. Kind yet tenacious, she was a pillar in her community.

"A HURRICANE, IN ITS PERFECT POWER...

OR THE CLIMBING, FALLING COLORS OF A RAINBOW."

GRANDMOTHER

A highly educated neighbor, Mrs. Bertha Flowers, became a mentor. She invited Maya to visit every week for tea and sent her home with armfuls of books. Maya learned to love the dance of words on the page. As she memorized poems and recited her favorites aloud, she found use for her voice again. She loved the authors who spoke of the despair and hope familiar to her.

DICKENS
tale of two cities

edgar allan POE

Frances Harper

JESSIE FAUSET

DURING THOSE YEARS IN STAMPS, I MET AND FELL IN LOVE WITH WILLIAM SHAKESPEARE.

the Merchant of VENICE
Shakespeare

When she was 14, Maya and her brother moved to San Francisco to live with their mother. Maya received a scholarship for drama and dance at the California Labor School. She was entranced by the city lights, the hills crisscrossed with cable cars, and the characters who swirled through her mother's home. Loud jazz rang from the record player—a constant backdrop.

OREGON

CALIFORNIA

NEVADA

San Francisco

Vivian Baxter taught her daughter to pursue her goals and push past any obstacles. However, when Maya became the first female black trolley conductor at the age of 16, her mother feared for her safety. On every route—even the four a.m. ones—Vivian drove behind with her shotgun on the passenger seat in case of trouble.

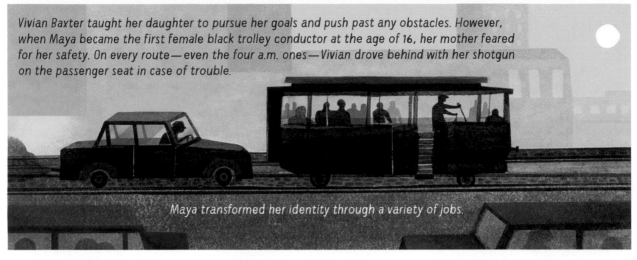

Maya transformed her identity through a variety of jobs.

She starred in the movie musical *Calypso Heat Wave*.

She became a civil rights activist, fundraiser, and coordinator.

She worked as a journalist and newspaper editor abroad.

James Baldwin, a renowned author and poet, was dazzled by Maya's storytelling skills. He dared her to publish an autobiography. Initially Maya laughed at the idea, but when she heard that a memoir was the hardest thing an author could attempt, the challenge motivated her. After writing for two years, she published her book. *I Know Why the Caged Bird Sings* landed on the bestseller list and remained there for several years.

Writing about personal experience was a way Maya could heal her past. Over a lifetime, she wrote seven volumes of memoirs. She also wrote scripts for plays and television.

Whenever she needed to focus, Maya would rent a hotel room. She would have the pictures removed from the walls and then lie in the bed, writing on big yellow notepads.

Her willingness to share her own stories with the world led Maya to cross paths with writers, activists, and political leaders. Oprah Winfrey considered Maya to be a mentor.

Maya said, "WHEN YOU LEARN, TEACH. WHEN YOU GET, GIVE." She lived by those words. And one day, the very same little girl who couldn't finish a poem in church without bursting into tears grew into the woman who would stand in the White House reciting a poem of her own . . . with the whole world watching.

"LOOK AT ME! LOOK AT ME!
LOOK AT ME NOW!
IT IS FUN TO
HAVE FUN
BUT YOU
HAVE TO
KNOW
HOW."

—*The Cat in the Hat*

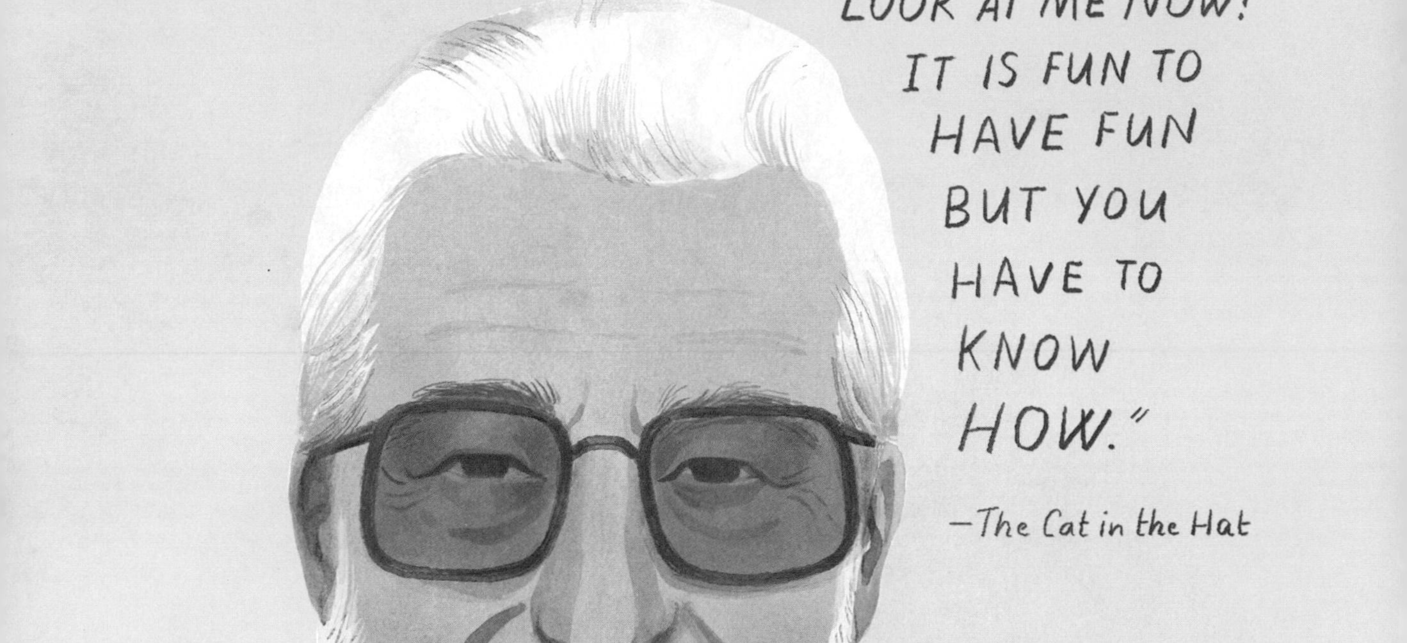

DR. SEUSS

- **1904** Born in Springfield, Massachusetts
- **1957** Publishes *The Cat in the Hat* and *How the Grinch Stole Christmas!*
- **1960** Publishes *Green Eggs and Ham*
- **1971** Publishes *The Lorax*
- **1990** Publishes *Oh, the Places You'll Go!*
- **1991** Dies in La Jolla, California

"I can't draw things the way that they are. I just get at the soul of things."

Born Theodor Seuss Geisel in Springfield, Massachusetts . . .

this boy would grow up to transform the field of early-reader books with this motto:

LESS WORK, MORE FUN!

Known as Ted, he had a childhood he would have preferred to forget. During World War I, classmates bullied Ted and his sister because of their German heritage.

Life improved after their father became a parks commissioner. The children were able to visit Forest Park Zoo as often as they liked. Ted drew exaggerated versions of the animals.

GIRAFFE
SNAKES

When his sister teased him, he drew his creatures all over her bedroom walls.

He did not find much support at school, where one art teacher remarked,

T.S.G.

YOU WILL NEVER LEARN TO DRAW... JUST SKIP THIS CLASS FOR THE REST OF THE TERM.

HA HAH HA haa

But Ted transformed the criticism into a stroke of luck. He never quit drawing, and over time it was this very lack of formal art education that shaped his distinctive "Seuss style."

SINCE I CAN'T DRAW, I'VE TAKEN THE AWKWARDNESS AND PECULIARITIES... AND DEVELOPED THEM.

In college, Ted edited and illustrated a humor magazine called *Jack-O-Lantern*. Some of his cartoons would later become the main characters of his children's books. He studied literature, intent on becoming a professor. One day, a classmate questioned his seemingly illogical plan. Ted followed her advice and, later, married her.

He would try many pen names before arriving at Dr. Seuss.

Ted illustrated ads for a pest control company. He became famous for his depictions of evil insects. His first idea for a children's book came as a complete surprise—while crossing the ocean by ship, he found himself listening to the peculiar rhythm of the engine. Rhyming words in the form of a story began to dance through his mind.

And to Think That I Saw It on Mulberry Street resulted, named after a place in his hometown. After the book received 25 rejections, Ted was ready to throw it away. Luckily, he bumped into a friend on the street who had become an editor for Vanguard Press . . . a book contract was drawn up that very same day.

When World War II began, Ted drew political cartoons denouncing fascism, and eventually joined the army to become head of its animation department. He used his talents to create training films for new soldiers, with a good dose of humor.

After the war, Ted and his wife collaborated on a film screenplay. *The 5,000 Fingers of Dr. T* featured a crazed music teacher and 150 students wearing five-fingered hats.

Ted made time to write for children again. In these postwar books, he added a moral dimension.

THE LORAX → CONSERVATION

THE BUTTER BATTLE BOOK → TOLERANCE

YERTLE THE TURTLE → EQUALITY

His books for early readers brought him the most recognition—yet he claimed they were the hardest to write. *The Cat in the Hat* story involved only 236 different words, but Ted labored for more than a year before he was satisfied.

Green Eggs and Ham followed, based on a dare. Ted's publisher bet him $50 that he couldn't write a book with just 50 vocabulary words. After sweating through numerous revisions, the tale about a picky eater and a ridiculous breakfast ensued. It was an instant hit.

Ted maintained his playful outlook at every age. He collected goofy hats in a secret closet and brought them out at parties. When Ted and his wife were unable to have children, they decided to invent a family.

Signatures of the children's names appeared on holiday cards to friends, and one of Ted's books was even dedicated to "Chrysanthemum Pearl," a favorite imaginary daughter.

Into his seventies, Ted showed no signs of slowing down—he created stories for television and wrote a rock opera. Though he never completed his novel for grownups, he wrote a picture book with them in mind: *You're Only Old Once!* After his death, Dr. Seuss was awarded a star on the Hollywood Walk of Fame. His stories remain popular today, with translations in more than 20 languages and book sales totaling more than 600 million copies.

Where did his endless ideas come from? Dr. Seuss joked:

"I GET ALL MY IDEAS IN SWITZERLAND, NEAR THE FORKA PASS. THERE IS A LITTLE TOWN CALLED GLETCH, AND 2,000 FEET UP ABOVE GLETCH THERE IS A SMALLER HAMLET CALLED ÜBER GLETCH. I GO THERE ON THE FOURTH OF AUGUST EVERY SUMMER TO GET MY CUCKOO CLOCK REPAIRED. WHILE THE CUCKOO IS IN THE HOSPITAL, I WANDER AROUND AND TALK TO THE PEOPLE IN THE STREETS. THEY ARE VERY STRANGE PEOPLE, AND I GET ALL MY IDEAS FROM THEM."

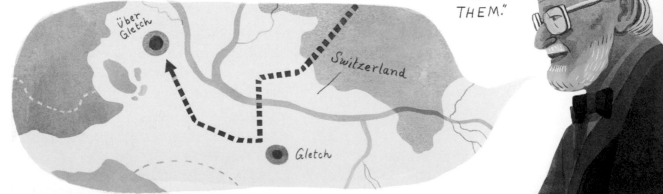

"PERHAPS ALL MEMORY IS A CHANCE AT STORYTELLING AND EVERY STORY BRINGS US CLOSER TO REVEALING OURSELVES TO OURSELVES."

— *A House of My Own*

SANDRA CISNEROS

1954
Born in Chicago, Illinois

1980
Publishes first book: *Bad Boys*, a poetry collection

1984
Publishes *The House on Mango Street*

1991
Publishes *Woman Hollering Creek and Other Stories*

2015
Publishes memoir, *A House of My Own*

The only sister among six brothers, Sandra Cisneros was born in 1954 in Chicago. Her father, an immigrant from Mexico City, regularly took his family to visit relatives in his hometown and raised his children in a dual-language home.

From early on, Sandra found her sense of belonging in the world of books. She recalled loving the picture book about a house that remains the same while everything changes around it.

At first, Sandra wrote only in secret. With so many brothers, it was hard to find a quiet corner in the house. She preferred to read tales from bygone eras, which gave her a sense of traveling to faraway places.

The Chicago Public Library, with its shelves and hallways of books, felt like a magical time machine to other worlds.

Sandra's mother, Elvira, was an avid reader and museum-goer . . . a "self-educator."

She encouraged Sandra to make her own way in the world using the skills of her mind.

Although Sandra had written her first poem at the age of 10, her writing didn't receive recognition until a high school teacher mentored her. She preferred writing after dark, to avoid interruption.

"My father would call me *Vampira* for writing at night.

I couldn't tell him that the night was my own private house."

After college, she attended the two-year Iowa Writers' Workshop to further her studies in fiction writing. It took time for Sandra to find her voice. At first, she felt intimidated when she noticed the differences between her own upbringing and the more privileged backgrounds of her fellow writers.

MY CLASSMATES WERE FROM THE BEST SCHOOLS IN THE COUNTRY.

THEY HAD BEEN BRED AS FINE HOTHOUSE FLOWERS.

I WAS A YELLOW WEED AMONG THE CITY'S CRACKS.

She finally decided to write about something close to her heart: the struggle for identity between conflicting cultures. Sandra wrote about her childhood, her neighbors, her town.

Upon her graduation, Sandra moved back to Chicago, where she taught former high school dropouts at the Latino Alternative High School.

She began work on a manuscript that combined her own experiences with stories told to her by her students about their own lives.

The resulting book, *The House on Mango Street*, was a form of "true fiction."

The book boldly portrayed gender inequality and the challenges of cultural minorities. To her surprise, the book struck a chord far beyond the Chicano community.

Sandra continued to teach. There were many aspiring writers who wanted to hear what she had to say.

Growing up between overlapping cultures gave her two ways of looking at the world. Sandra combined both languages to add rhythm and spice to her writing.

"I AM BEYOND THE JAW OF LAW. I'M *LA DESPERADA*, MOST-WANTED PUBLIC ENEMY. MY HAPPY PICTURE, GRINNING FROM THE WALL."

WANTED:

Woman Hollering Creek and other stories

1995

CARAMELO 1998

a Memoir: 2015

A HOUSE OF MY OWN

More publications followed: collections of essays, poems, short stories, and several novels.

Sandra now lives alone in a home she views as her "writing sanctuary." When asked why she has chosen not to have children, Sandra says:

"I'VE NEVER SEEN A MARRIAGE THAT IS AS HAPPY AS MY LIVING ALONE. MY WRITING IS MY CHILD AND I DON'T WANT ANYTHING TO COME BETWEEN US."

In her advice to young writers, Sandra stresses the importance of setting the right mood.

"TALK ABOUT YOUR PIECE OF WRITING IN THE LANGUAGE YOU WOULD USE IF YOU WERE WEARING YOUR PAJAMAS AND YOU WERE SEATED AT A TABLE WITH YOUR VERY GOOD FRIEND...

"WHEN YOU EDIT, YOU IMAGINE YOUR ENEMY IS SEATED ON THE OTHER SIDE OF THE TABLE... SO YOU ARE GOING TO POLISH, AND REVISE, AND REWRITE, AND CUT OUT, AND SHAPE IT, SO THAT YOUR ENEMY HAS NO PLACE TO GRIP IT."

"NEVER DO ANYTHING BY HALVES IF YOU WANT TO GET AWAY WITH IT. BE OUTRAGEOUS. GO THE WHOLE HOG."
—Matilda

ROALD DAHL

1916
Born in Llandaff, Wales

1964
Publishes *Charlie and the Chocolate Factory*

1970
Publishes *Fantastic Mr. Fox*

1982
Publishes *The BFG*

1990
Dies in Oxford and is buried in Buckinghamshire, England

Destined to become an adventurer, Roald Dahl was born in Llandaff, Wales, to Norwegian parents. He was named after Roald Amundsen—the first explorer to reach the South Pole.

Roald delighted in his moments of independence. Wheeling around country roads on his tricycle, he raced to the candy store at every chance he had.

Presuming all children to be ill-behaved thieves the store's owner tormented Roald to no end. After discovering a dead rodent, a plan for revenge formed in Roald's mind.

He dubbed it the Great Mouse Plot. After sneaking the rotten animal into a jar of gobstoppers, he was caught and punished. However, his prank earned him the admiration of fellow classmates. Later, Roald was sent to boarding school—not as a punishment, though it felt as such, to him.

Terribly homesick, Roald promptly escaped by faking appendicitis.

For his mother's sake, he returned to school and endured the strict rules, harsh consequences, and rampant bullying.

HURRY UP, DAHL.

Homesick, he wrote letters to his mother every Sunday. (She saved every one, more than 600 by the end of her life.)

Roald's bizarre writing style was often met with criticism. One teacher wrote,

ROALD DAHL REPORT:
I have never met a boy who so persistently writes the exact opposite of what he means.

His earliest stories gave a glimpse into his unusual imagination. One tale featured a machine that turned into conversations from the past.

Roald kept many secret diaries and went to great lengths to hide them. One he kept in a cookie tin zipped into a toiletries bag and hung from the tallest branch of a tree.

Since he loved to read, Roald's mother sent comics to him at school. At home, he read and reread every volume in the encyclopedia set.

Throughout Roald's life, candy remained an ongoing inspiration and obsession.

As a young child, he spent every penny he had on Licorice Bootlaces, Sherbet Suckers, and Pear Drops.

At school, when the Cadbury chocolate factory sent samples for students to test, Roald was in heaven. He rated his favorite flavors, from Milk Flake to Lemon Marshmallow.

Even as an adult, he stashed an emergency supply of gumdrops under his bed.

"I BEGAN TO REALIZE THAT THE LARGE CHOCOLATE COMPANIES ACTUALLY DID POSSESS INVENTING ROOMS AND THEY TOOK THEIR INVENTING SERIOUSLY... I USED TO IMAGINE MYSELF WORKING IN ONE OF THESE LABS..."

After school, he declined college in favor of travel. He longed for encounters with dangerous wildlife and foreign cultures. A sales position at an oil company brought both his way. After a few years of experience, he was assigned a post in East Africa.

In Tanzania, Roald encountered lions, crocodiles, and black mamba snakes—just as he hoped.

World War II interrupted and Roald enlisted in the Royal Air Force. After one day of training, he flew solo.

He survived a harrowing crash. Luckily, this event would later help launch his writing career.

After recovering from injuries, Roald returned home and met an actress, whom she married.

GIPSY HOUSE

He continued to work for the air force in various noncombat positions—all were eventually dissatisfying.

SHOT DOWN OVER LIBYA

Not until the renowned author C. S. Forester convinced Roald to write about his experiences in war did he consider publishing as a career.

As he began writing for magazines, Roald tested his more imaginative storytelling on his own children.

At their bedside, he spun wild tales of ogres and giants while serving up glasses of "witches' potion" (milk tinted green with food coloring).

ALMA

CHOPPER

Often, Roald cast the family pets as side characters: dogs, chickens, ponies, a goat, and a tortoise.

When a screenwriting job was canceled, Roald found time to finish an old idea he'd had for a children's book. Wishing to avoid stereotypical heroes, he wrote about a timid boy who befriends giant insects.

JAMES AND THE GIANT PEACH

Sales were initially slow in the United States because of bad reviews. However, a later reprint in England immediately sold out, and Roald's reputation as a writer received a boost.

His boyhood obsession with candy inspired his next book, *Charlie and the Chocolate Factory*. Roald lived out his fantasy of owning a candy empire on the pages.

Roald scribbled the beginnings of stories in his "Ideas Book," where a character might exist for years before a plot formed. Often, he wrote too many characters into a story and had to cut several out as he edited.

As scraps from the Ideas Book became full-fledged tales, more heroes and antiheroes emerged in Roald's best-selling books.

He also wrote two memoirs: *Boy*, about his childhood, and *Going Solo*, recounting his daring feats as a pilot.

1970 FANTASTIC MR. FOX

1975 DANNY, THE CHAMPION OF THE WORLD

1980

1982 THE BFG

THE TWITS

1988 MATILDA

Roald always dreaded the moment after a book was finished. He kept worrying that it might be his last good idea and his career as a writer would come to an abrupt end.

The Big Friendly Giant was Roald's favorite tale. He had acted out the story when his kids were young, "blowing dreams" in their window at bedtime.

Even at Roald's gravesite, his favorite character lives on. Visitors to his museum can follow giant cement footprints leading to the place where Roald is buried.

ROALD DAHL

In his lifetime, Roald harbored a great many writing quirks and opinions.

He built a hut in the garden where he wrote alone, on yellow legal pads. Discarded drafts were burned in monthly bonfires.

He hoped to grab the reader's attention with the first sentence of each story. He always wrote titles last.

MATILDA

To Roald, writing seemed like hard work. When asked about his process, he quipped,

"WRITING IS MAINLY PERSPIRATION, NOT INSPIRATION!"

"BUT HE UNDERSTOOD AT LAST WHAT DUMBLEDORE HAD BEEN TRYING TO TELL HIM. IT WAS, HE THOUGHT, THE DIFFERENCE BETWEEN BEING DRAGGED INTO THE ARENA TO FACE A BATTLE TO THE DEATH AND WALKING INTO THE ARENA WITH YOUR HEAD HELD HIGH."

—*Harry Potter and the Half-Blood Prince*

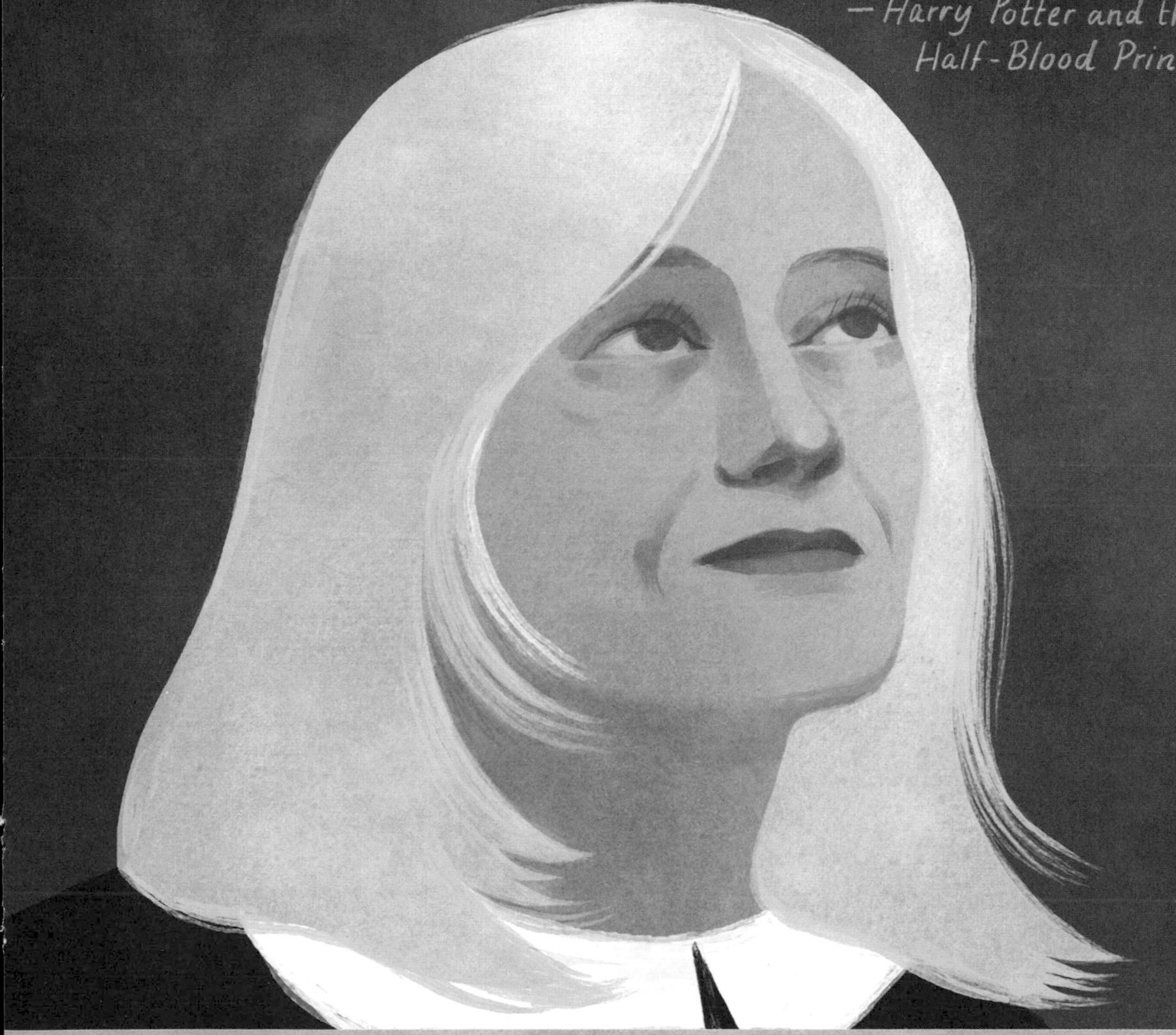

J. K. ROWLING

1965
Born in Gloucestershire, England

1997
Publishes *Harry Potter and the Sorcerer's Stone* in the United States

1998–2007
Publishes six more books in the Harry Potter series

2012
Publishes *The Casual Vacancy*

2015
Publishes commencement speech titled "Very Good Lives: The Fringe Benefits of Failure and the Importance of Imagination"

Born in Gloucestershire, in South West England, Joanne Rowling showed an early interest in storytelling as a child. However, it would be a long time before she confided her secret dream of becoming a writer to anyone.

At age six, she spun her first tale about a rabbit who was sick in bed with the measles.

In the story, the rabbit's neighbor—a giant insect named "Miss Bee"—drops by to cheer him up.

"AND SINCE THAT TIME, I HAVE WANTED TO BE A WRITER, THOUGH I RARELY TOLD ANYONE SO. I WAS AFRAID THEY'D TELL ME I DIDN'T HAVE A HOPE."

Ordinary details from Joanne's childhood reappeared later in the fantastical settings of her books: the nearby train station, a hidden cupboard under the stairs, the woods near the cottage where her family moved when she was nine (known as the Forest of Dean).

Wandering alone among those trees, Joanne felt the paradox of wild places: deep calm beneath a surface of eerie chills. This setting provided the inspiration for the "Forbidden Forest"—the woods behind the wizarding school attended by Harry Potter.

Stories were always a family priority, with books piled up in every room of the house.

Joanne loved Manxmouse by Paul Gallico, about a tiny creature—part opossum, rabbit, kangaroo, and mouse—who must evade the dreadful Manx Cat.

The Little White Horse by Elizabeth Goudge was another influence. Later, Joanne treasured the Chronicles of Narnia by C. S. Lewis and Emma by Jane Austen.

Jo March from Little Women was the literary heroine with whom she most identified. Besides sharing the same name, they both had a hot temper and a burning ambition to become a writer.

At school, Joanne's daydreaming clashed with the rigor of schedules. Burdened by thick glasses, freckles, and a lack of skill at sports, she aligned with the other misfits and bookworms.

As a shy teenager, she often refrained from class discussions. Upon graduation, when students voted on who was most likely to succeed, or to become a millionaire, Joanne received the dubious honor of the student who was least likely to go to jail.

These years were darkened by her mother's diagnosis with a serious disease. Joanne's retreat into writing became her only thread of constancy. The same year that Jo began drafting her very first version of Harry Potter's wizarding world, her mother died.

The idea for Harry Potter had originally come to her during a stalled train ride. As she gazed out the window, waiting for the train to start, the image of a boy appeared in her mind.

He was traveling to Wizarding School on a magical train—invisible to ordinary humans. Joanne borrowed a pen and quickly jotted notes onto a napkin.

She used every spare moment to write about her idea: early mornings, late nights . . . and often on the go while traveling.

The names of the houses of Hogwarts came to her while on a plane, with only an (unused) air sickness bag to write on.

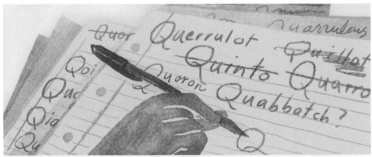

Not everything came as easily—Jo once filled five notebook pages with Q words before finally arriving at Quidditch, the favored sport of wizards and witches.

After her mother's death, Joanne's life became increasingly difficult. As a young adult, she tried several short-term jobs as her brief marriage unraveled. She had moved to a foreign country and, after her divorce, she returned home without much of a plan.

Struggling as an unemployed single mom, Joanne sank into a period of clinical depression.

In 1993, she spent Christmas in Edinburgh, Scotland, with her sister, living on welfare benefits while she finished *Harry Potter and the Sorcerer's Stone* on an old typewriter.

After the book's completion, it received many rejections from publishers. At last, Jo received a letter of acceptance in the mail.

HARRY POTTER
J.K. ROWLING

Seven long years had passed from the very moment Harry Potter appeared as an idea until the day Jo held her published book. Even then, she was discouraged from writing as a career. Her first publisher famously said, "You'll never make any money out of children's books, Jo."

Two years later, Jo made her first million in royalties. The Harry Potter series broke every sales record in publishing history. Joanne wrote follow-up plays and guidebooks for the world of Harry Potter. A theme park based on the book opened in Florida in 2010.

Joanne's success hasn't erased the memory of her difficult beginnings. When young writers inquire, she often gives tough advice:

YOU JUST HAVE TO RESIGN YOURSELF TO WASTING A LOT OF TREES BEFORE YOU WRITE ANYTHING REALLY GOOD.

THAT'S JUST HOW IT IS.

"SOMETIMES, A FIGHT YOU CANNOT WIN IS STILL WORTH FIGHTING."
— The Shadow Hero

楊謹倫 GENE LUEN YANG

1973
Born in the Bay Area, California

1997
Self-publishes Gordon Yamamoto and the King of the Geeks

2006
Publishes American Born Chinese

2013
Publishes graphic novel set: Boxers and Saints

2017
Writes New Super-Man series with DC Comics

> *"ACTUALLY, MORE OF US FEEL LIKE OUTSIDERS THAN INSIDERS. IN A WEIRD WAY, THAT KIND OF TIES US ALL TOGETHER."*

Gene Luen Yang was born in California, a first-generation Asian American. His parents emigrated separately from Hong Kong and Taiwan, and met, auspiciously, in a college library.

As a young child, Gene dreamed of becoming a Disney animator. His parents weren't thrilled. In fifth grade, Gene discovered comics. His obsession with superheroes eclipsed everything.

He spent all his hours doodling and announced his plan to become a cartoonist . . . to his parents' dismay. They shared his love of stories but worried it would be a terrible career choice.

Undaunted by his parents' reactions, Gene went into business with a grade-school friend, creating their own superhero tales. The kids photocopied their comics and sold them at school. This gave Gene an early taste for self-publishing, which he would try again later.

Heading into his teen years, Gene admits he was a "standard-issue nerd": an unathletic asthma sufferer, obsessed with computer programming and collecting comics.

With only a few other Chinese students at school, Gene found junior high to be a gauntlet of anxiety. As he walked through the hallways, racial slurs echoed behind him. He worried that everyone felt the same as the bullies.

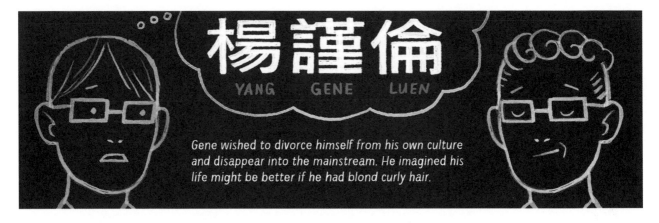

楊謹倫

YANG   GENE   LUEN

Gene wished to divorce himself from his own culture and disappear into the mainstream. He imagined his life might be better if he had blond curly hair.

In high school, Gene tried sports. He enjoyed being part of a team, despite all his efforts yielding little to no improvement. Later, Gene joked that he learned the "art of persistence" by continuing to do something he lacked the natural talent for.

It wasn't until college that Gene found himself surrounded by many other classmates who were immigrants and children of immigrants. He began to identify as Asian American for the first time.

"I STARTED BEING ABLE TO EXPLAIN AND UNDERSTAND THE DISCOMFORT I HAD FELT SINCE I WAS A KID. THIS EXPERIENCE OF FEELING LIKE AN OUTSIDER WASN'T UNIQUE TO ME. IT WAS ACTUALLY A VERY COMMON THING."

In college, Gene focused on computer engineering. After he had graduated and worked in the field for two years, Gene took a silent retreat to think over his future.

?

hello, class!

Afterward, he felt moved to quit his job and teach computer science at a high school. Spending time with teenagers reminded him of his youthful ambitions to make comics.

GORDON YAMAMOTO AND THE KING OF THE GEEKS
GENE YANG

Gene self-published under his own imprint, Humble Comics. His first story won him the Xeric Foundation grant.

AMERICAN BORN CHINESE
by GENE Y

Winning this prize for self-published comic book creators encouraged Gene to develop a more personal tale about his outsider experience.

The book interlaced three tales: an Asian American boy who feels out of place in a new school; the Chinese Monkey King, based on stories Gene's mother had told him; and Chin-Kee, a figure who embodied negative racial stereotypes.

Gene photocopied and stapled the series, distributing the copies himself.

"I REMEMBER THINKING, 'I'LL NEVER BE ABLE TO MAKE ANY MONEY OFF THIS. I'LL JUST DO IT BECAUSE I LOVE IT.'"

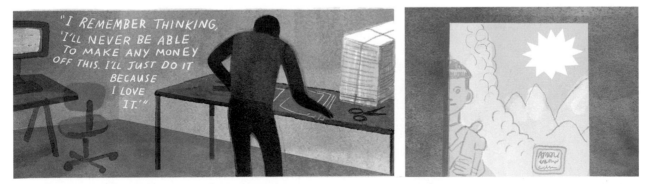

First Second Books, a graphic novel imprint, saw the book's potential and offered Gene a contract. The book became a bestseller and garnered several awards, along with new opportunities.

He spent six years on his next project—a two-volume work of historical fiction, based upon China's Boxer Rebellion.

Gene also paired up with various artists to write serial stories for Dark Horse and DC Comics. By collaborating with illustrators, he could focus on his writing.

In 2016, Gene was appointed the National Ambassador for Young People's Literature—he was the first graphic novelist to receive this honor. A sought-after speaker, Gene traveled the world to spread empathy through stories. He continued to teach by day and create stories by night, living the double life common to many superheroes.

Recently he has written a comics series about coders who use logic puzzles and programming skills to solve mysteries.

On his central focus:

STORY IS ABOUT TENSION... ABOUT CONFLICT. SINCE I'VE FELT TENSION BETWEEN ME AS AN INDIVIDUAL AND MY COMMUNITY SO DEEPLY, IT COMES OUT IN MY STORIES.

On choosing the graphic novel format:

WORDS AND IMAGES CONVEY EMOTION DIFFERENTLY... I WANTED TO ATTACK STEREOTYPES THROUGH IMAGE BECAUSE I WANTED YOU TO FEEL IT IN YOUR GUT.

"ONCE UPON A TIME THERE WERE FOUR LITTLE RABBITS, FLOPSY, MOPSY, COTTON-TAIL, AND PETER. THEY LIVED WITH THEIR MOTHER IN A SAND-BANK UNDERNEATH THE ROOT OF A VERY BIG FIR-TREE."

—*The Tale of Peter Rabbit*

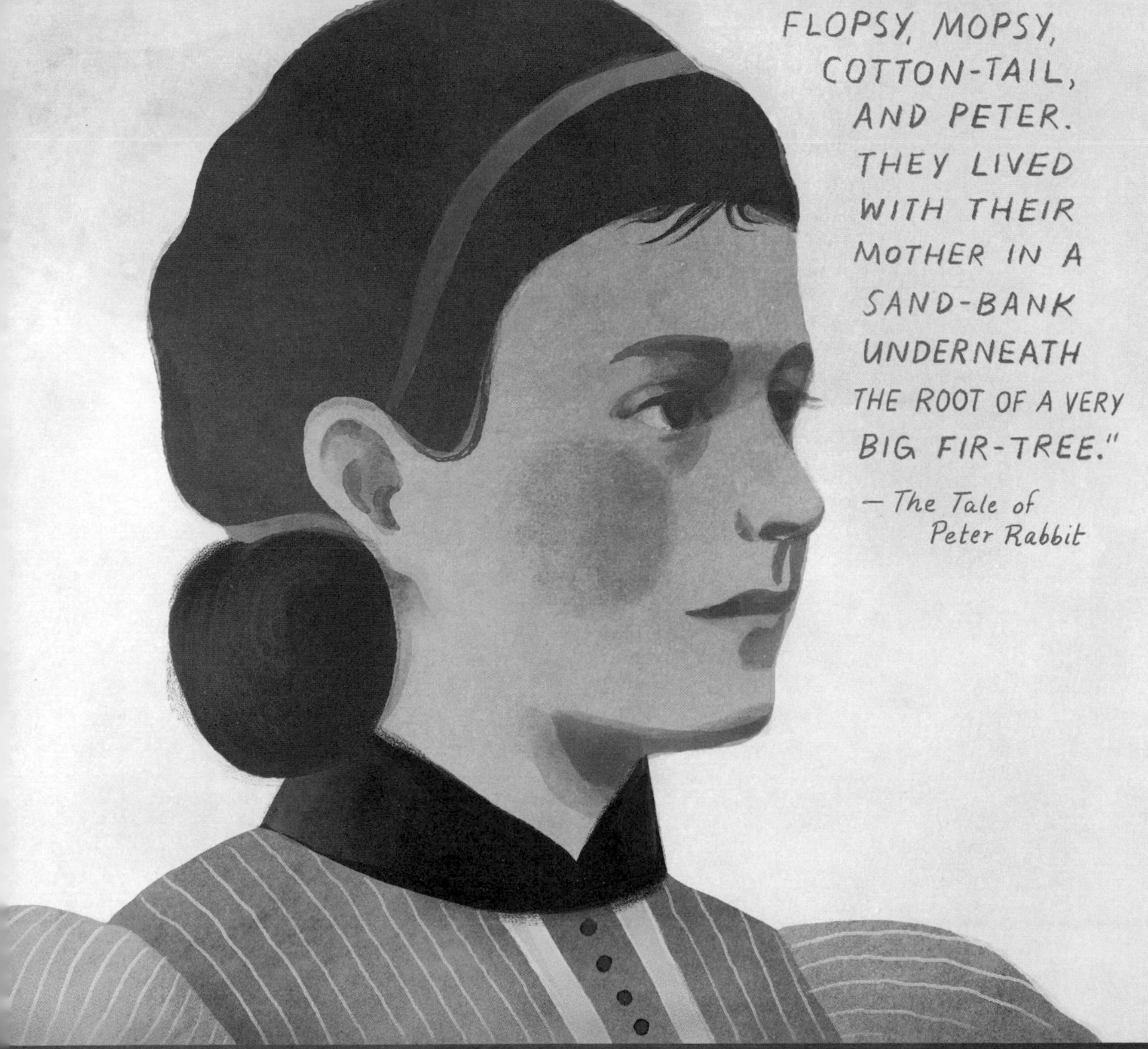

BEATRIX POTTER

1866
Born in London, England

1901
Self-publishes *The Tale of Peter Rabbit*

1902–1930
Warne & Co. reprints *Peter Rabbit* and publishes 22 more books

1939
Establishes wildlife preservation area

1943
Dies at Castle Cottage, in Near Sawrey, England

Born in England during an era when it was unusual for women to write, Beatrix Potter would shatter the expectations of her time. Besides her acclaim as a storyteller, she would add entrepreneur, scientific illustrator, farm owner, and wildlife conservationist to her list of titles.

Many famous authors who followed later in history have cited her as one of their most important inspirations.

Beatrix grew up in the big city of London but felt at home only in the Scottish countryside, where her family vacationed. With only her baby brother and governess for company, Beatrix was often lonely. Except for holidays, she spent most of her childhood in the nursery.

She found friends within the pages of books. Studying all manner of fables and fairy tales, she copied the characters into her sketchbook.

Deeply influenced by the Brer Rabbit tales of Uncle Remus, she meticulously hand-lettered the stories and illustrated them with her watercolor set.

Beatrix spent much of her time with a menagerie of pets. She painted them from life, naming each and inventing stories about them to entertain her family. Her favorite rabbit, Benjamin Bouncer, was trained to follow her on a leash and later provided inspiration for the Peter Rabbit tales.

The nursery was something of a zoo. Animals roamed freely: dogs, kittens, guinea pigs, and wild mice (that had been tamed). Beatrix also captured reptiles and insects for her collection.

On summer trips, Beatrix insisted on bringing all her pets, packed into baskets and boxes.

An ardent scientist, she set her emotions aside when pets died. She boiled the bones and recreated the skeletons for further study. Once, Beatrix stuffed and framed a rare species of bat with her own taxidermy kit. She painted her insects in microscopic detail.

During her teen years, Beatrix kept a journal in a secret code. She recorded her opinions about society and family life, often frustrated with the expectations of her mother. Mrs. Potter wished her daughter would care about social status rather than painting techniques.

Beatrix penned her most famous tale quite by accident. While writing to the sick child of her governess, she ran out of news and decided to invent a tale about a rabbit. She would illustrate many stories in her letters before she began to think of herself as an author.

With her brother, she founded a successful holiday card business, featuring animal characters dressed in top hats and bow ties. With the profits, Beatrix self-published her story about Peter Rabbit, printing 250 books to give away to family and friends.

A year earlier, the book had been turned down by several publishers, but Warne and Company decided to republish it after Beatrix agreed to color the black-and-white illustrations.

The little book attracted such widespread interest in its first year of publication that it was reprinted six times. At a prolific pace, Beatrix created 22 more stories over the next 30 years. Her tales sprang from memories of pets and observations of nature on her daily walks.

Fascinated by fungi, Beatrix collected and photographed her own specimens. She illustrated hundreds of them in scientific detail and penned theories about the secret life of spores. Since women were barred from scientific gatherings, her paper was presented on her behalf at the Linnean Society, a forum for natural history and taxonomy, by a fellow mycologist.

Since childhood, Beatrix had dreamed of living in the country. Unmarried and lacking the resources a husband would have provided, she'd been unable to afford her own place. Her parents pressured her to find a wealthy match, but when book sales skyrocketed, Beatrix was able to purchase a farm of her own.

Next, she expanded her artistic scope by creating Peter Rabbit merchandise—a rabbit doll, board game, and wallpaper with scenes from her books. Increased profits enabled her to purchase land surrounding the farm, protecting the space from urban development.

In her will, Beatrix bestowed her land to the National Trust, setting aside thousands of acres as a wilderness area, preserving the habitats of her beloved characters.

As to why she wrote, Beatrix claimed,

"I HAVE JUST MADE STORIES TO PLEASE MYSELF BECAUSE I NEVER GREW UP."

"'THIS IS THE LAND OF NARNIA', SAID THE FAUN,
'WHERE WE ARE NOW; ALL THAT LIES BETWEEN
THE LAMP-POST AND THE GREAT CASTLE OF
CAIR PARAVEL ON THE EASTERN SEA.'"
— The Lion, the Witch, and the Wardrobe

C. S. LEWIS

1898
Born in Belfast,
Northern Ireland

1919
Publishes first book of poetry,
Spirits in Bondage: A Cycle of Lyrics

1938-1945
Publishes Space
Trilogy

1950-1956
Publishes the
Chronicles of
Narnia

1955
Publishes memoir
Surprised by
Joy

1963
Dies in Oxford,
England

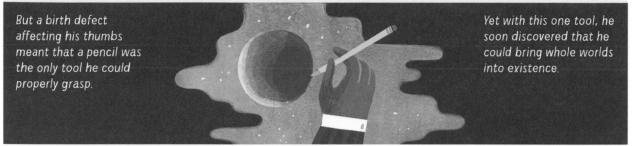

But a birth defect affecting his thumbs meant that a pencil was the only tool he could properly grasp.

Yet with this one tool, he soon discovered that he could bring whole worlds into existence.

Only after surviving boarding school, braving World War I, and navigating academia did C. S. Lewis discover that the things he truly wished to express could best be conveyed through children's books. His writing was influenced by memories of joy, longing, and magic from his childhood.

I will answer only to the name Jack.

When he was four, his little dog, Jacksie, died in a car accident. Filled with grief, the young boy changed his name to that of his beloved pet.

Fortunately, Jack found a lifelong friend in his older brother, Warren. The boys built forts together and read all the same books.

Their favorite tales involved talking animals, magical gardens, and adventures at sea. The brothers invented their own wonderlands and painted them into existence, creating elaborate maps.

One day, Warren made a toy garden out of an old tin box with moss and twigs. This gift sparked the imaginary "land of Boxen," which the boys would develop for years. Mice in chain-mail suits rode out to battle giant cats, and steamships sailed the oceans.

Their carefree days ended when Warren was sent to boarding school. Both boys were miserable—Jack, at home alone, and Warren, frustrated by the strict routines of school. Yet on holiday breaks, the brothers resumed work on their fantasy world.

Jack claimed the attic as his private study. He taped collages from magazines on the walls and surrounded himself with stacks of books. Using every color in his paint box, Jack continued work on the land of Boxen, where all his favorite things could keep him company.

"I am a product of long corridors, empty sunlit rooms...attics explored in solitude..."

A shadow descended over the house when Mrs. Lewis became gravely ill. Doctors came and went while time seemed to stand still. Jack was nine years old when his mother died.

With that loss, all sense of security unraveled.

The grieving father sent both boys to boarding school, where Jack endured snobs, bullies, and punishments. He sent letters begging to be released. After two years, Jack's wish was granted.

Upon returning home, he began private studies with the renowned scholar William Kirkpatrick. Jack flourished under the guidance of his new mentor.

Nicknamed by the family:
"THE GREAT KNOCK"

Epic poetry and Norse mythology were favorite topics. Jack's fascination with "Northernness"—the cold, vast spaces—would reappear in his Narnia series.

BALDER'S FUNERAL SHIP

As Jack began college at Oxford, World War I interrupted. He enlisted and fought in the army until an injury caused his discharge. Jack began writing poetry; some recounted his experiences of battle. After returning to Oxford, he began tutoring and was enveloped by writers, philosophers, and poets. Amid the exchange of minds, Jack found an anchor for his soul.

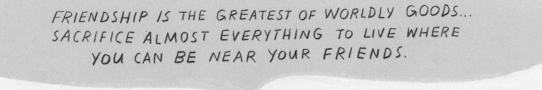

FRIENDSHIP IS THE GREATEST OF WORLDLY GOODS... SACRIFICE ALMOST EVERYTHING TO LIVE WHERE YOU CAN BE NEAR YOUR FRIENDS.

A small group of dedicated thinkers began an informal society dubbed the Inklings. They met every week at a local pub to share recent work. Honesty, praise, and criticism flowed freely. Lively discussions generated ideas for the next round of stories and essays. Members included Jack's older brother, Warren, an American poet named Joy Davidman (who later married Jack), and J.R.R. Tolkien, author of The Hobbit and the Lord of the Rings trilogy.

Jack's friendship with Tolkien would have the greatest impact on his work. As they discussed shared interests in theology and cosmology, Tolkien dared Jack to write a fantasy story. Both authors agreed to explore the science fiction genre—Jack would focus on interplanetary exploration while Tolkien would delve into time travel.

While his friend never finished his end of the bargain, Jack went on to create a sci-fi series known as the Space Trilogy.

Still, there were many things Jack wished to write about. Returning to his land of Boxen, he began to see the necessity of telling a children's fairy tale. At first, images appeared to him: a faun with an umbrella, a queen on a sledge, a magnificent lion. Then he began writing the Chronicles of Narnia, seven volumes in total.

It is winter in Narnia, and has been for ever so long...

Jack also wrote nonfiction books, essays, and memoirs. After the death of his wife, he recorded his dark journey of mourning in a final book, *A Grief Observed*.

Nearly half a century passed between the publication of the Chronicles of Narnia and his early idea from childhood. Jack has advised writers to keep all their writing.

"WHEN YOU GIVE UP ON A BIT OF WORK, DON'T THROW IT AWAY. PUT IT IN A DRAWER. IT MAY COME IN USEFUL LATER. MUCH OF MY BEST WORK... IS THE RE-WRITING OF THINGS BEGUN AND ABANDONED YEARS EARLIER."

"IT SEEMED TO TRAVEL WITH HER, TO SWEEP HER ALOFT IN THE POWER OF SONG, SO THAT SHE WAS MOVING IN GLORY AMONG THE STARS, AND FOR A MOMENT SHE, TOO, FELT THAT THE WORDS DARKNESS AND LIGHT HAD NO MEANING."

— A Wrinkle in Time

MADELEINE L'ENGLE

1918
Born in New York City

1945
Publishes
The Small Rain

1962
Publishes
A Wrinkle in Time

1973
Publishes
A Wind in the Door

1978
Publishes
A Swiftly Tilting Planet

1986
Publishes Many Waters

2007
Dies in Litchfield, Connecticut

The only child of a writer and a musician, Madeleine seemed destined to appreciate the lyrical, rhythmic beauty of the written word.

Her parents kept busy with their careers, so she turned to writing as a way of amusing herself. She wrote her first story at the age of five and kept a journal from the age of eight. However, these early efforts were not recognized at school. More than once, teachers mistook her awkwardness for stupidity.

It was a dark and stormy night...

Her clumsiness made her unpopular in the schoolyard. Madeleine was often the last one picked for sports.

She retreated into a world of her own, writing stories and getting lost in her favorite books.

The characters seemed so alive; Madeleine soared and sank with their triumphs and plights.

Madeleine's parents disagreed about education. She was shuffled from one school to another.

Entranced by mythology, Madeleine read ancient tales from around the globe. Her love of Shakespeare inspired her to try acting in high school, where a teacher noticed her talent and encouraged further studies.

Madeleine studied drama in college, and afterward worked in theater. Acting paid the bills while she wrote in the early-morning hours. Two of her novels were finally published—and yet a career in writing seemed distant.

A romance with a fellow actor led to marriage and three young children. Madeleine set aside acting to raise her family in a rural town where cows outnumbered the people.

During this time, Madeleine discovered Einstein and became intrigued by his Theory of Relativity.

$E = mc^2$
ENERGY = MASS × SPEED OF LIGHT

> TIME
slope = SPEED OF LIGHT

PAST
← EVENT
FUTURE

$M = $
WAVE LENGTH

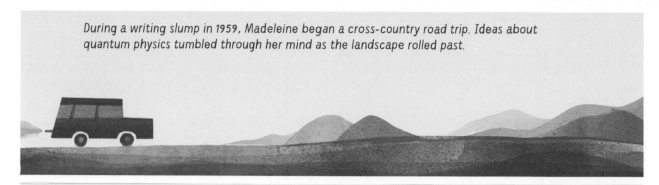

During a writing slump in 1959, Madeleine began a cross-country road trip. Ideas about quantum physics tumbled through her mind as the landscape rolled past.

"We drove through a world of deserts and buttes and leafless mountains... Suddenly into my mind came the names MRS. WHATSIT, MRS. WHO, MRS. WHICH."

As soon as she reached home, Madeleine began to write.

A Wrinkle in Time featured fantastical themes, such as time travel and cosmology. After 26 rejections, it was finally published. The book broke several taboos: the protagonist was female, the subjects were considered too complex for children, and the scope made it tricky to label as science fiction or fantasy. Against these odds, the book won the Newbery Medal.

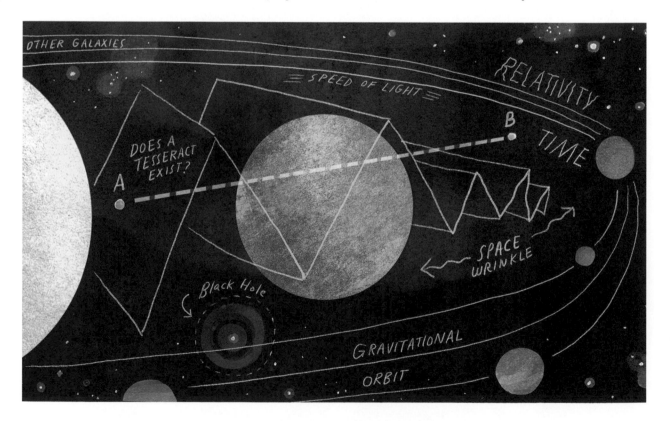

Fame didn't make things easy—A Wrinkle in Time was banned in a number of cities. Many adults had a hard time understanding the things that children easily embraced.

For some children, the book sparked new ideas about their own future possibilities.

The astronaut Janice Voss was inspired to study astrophysics while reading the novel in grade school.

After she was hired by NASA, Janice wrote to Madeleine, asking if she could bring a copy of *A Wrinkle in Time* with her on a mission. It became one of the first books to enter outer space.

Over the next 20 years, more books followed as a series, the Time Quintet, featuring adventures in cellular biology and the concept of nonlinear time.

"I AVOIDED SCIENCE IN SCHOOL AS MUCH AS POSSIBLE...[BUT I] READ IT FOR MYSELF, NOT FOR SCHOOL. I FOUND IT FASCINATING THAT LIGHT IS A PARTICLE AND THAT IT IS ALSO A STRAIGHT LINE."

Since the beginning of the Time Quintet, hundreds of fan letters arrived every week.

The youngest writers asked the toughest questions, seeking her perspective on life, death, and moral purpose.

When asked to define science fiction, Madeleine replied, "Isn't EVERYTHING?"

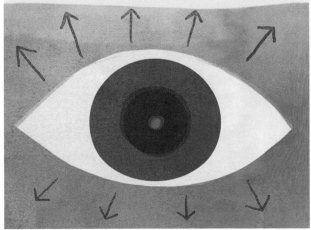

SOURCE NOTES

MARK TWAIN

12 "I was incapacitated": Kolb, *Mark Twain*, p. 75.
13 "Doors open at 7": Fleischman, *The Trouble Begins*, p. 138.
14 "[Tom] was ignorant": Twain, *Autobiography of Mark Twain*, vol. 1, p. 276.
   "Life would be": Phelps, *Autobiography, with Letters*, Letter to George Bainton,
         October 15, 1888.
   "The difference between": Twain Quotes. "Mark Twain Quotations—Difference,"
      www.twainquotes.com/Difference.html, accessed March 12, 2018.

MAYA ANGELOU

16 "Bailey was the greatest": Angelou, *Caged Bird*, p. 23.
   "My obsession with pineapples": Ibid., p. 17.
   "I could crawl": Johnson, *The Very Best of Maya Angelou*, p. 14.
17 "a hurricane, in": Angelou, *Caged Bird*, p. 98.
   "During those years": Ibid., p. 11.
19 "When you learn": Lynn Okura, "Maya Angelou Master Class," *Huffington Post*,
         May 30, 2014.
   "The horizon leans": Jose R. Lopez, "Maya Angelou: 'On the Pulse of Morning,'"
      New York Times, January 21, 1993.

DR. SEUSS

21 "I can't draw things": Hilliard Harper, "The Private World of Dr. Seuss: A Visit to Theodor
Geisel's La Jolla Mountaintop," *Los Angeles Times*, May 25, 1986.

"You will never": "Theodor Seuss Geisel," *Major Authors and Illustrators for Children and
Young Adults*, Gale, a Cengage Company, 2002, *Biography in Context*, http://
ic.galegroup.com/ic/bic1/ReferenceDetailsPage/ReferenceDetailsWindow?display
GroupName=Reference&zid=986b0cc501325802bba4c8c541e7793a&p=BIC1&action=
2&catId=GALE%7C00000000MRJB&documentId=GALE%7CK1617001313&source=Book
mark&u=morenetfznms&jsid=9b85aaa, accessed November 26, 2017.

"Since I can't draw": Ibid.

22 "That's a fine flying cow": Handy, *Wild Things*, p. 115.

24 "I get all my ideas": Nel, *Annotated Cat*, p. 26.

SANDRA CISNEROS

27 "My father would": Cisneros, *House of My Own*, p. 743.

"My classmates were": Warrick, *Sandra Cisneros*, p. 6.

29 "I've never seen": Pilar E. Aranda Rodriguez, "On the Solitary Fate of Being Mexican,
Female, Wicked, and Thirty-Three: An Interview with Sandra Cisneros," *Americas
Review* 18 (Spring 1990): 64–80.

"Talk about your piece": Ruth Behar, "Talking in Our Pajamas: A Conversation with
Sandra Cisneros on Finding Your Voice, Fear of Highways, Tacos, Travel, and the
Need for Peace in the World," *Michigan Quarterly Review* 47, no. 3 (2008).

ROALD DAHL

31 "I have never": Solomon, *Roald Dahl's Marvellous Medicine*, p. 63.

32 "I began to realize": Dahl, "Repton and Shell, 1929–36 (age 13–20): Chocolates," in *Boy:
Tales of Childhood*, Kindle edition.

34 "Writing is mainly perspiration" Cooling, *D Is for Dahl*, p. 117.

J. K. ROWLING

36 "And since that time": J. K. Rowling, "The Not Especially Fascinating Life So Far of J. K. Rowling," www.accio-quote.org/articles/1998/autobiography.html, accessed September 6, 2018.
37 Jo March from *Little Women*: "J. K. Rowling: By the Book," *New York Times*, October 11, 2012.
38 "I have never": Christopher Connors, "The Formula That Leads to Wild Success, Part 6: J. K. Rowling," *The Mission*, Medium.com, July 19, 2016.
39 "You just have to resign": Linda L. Richards, "Profiles: J. K. Rowling," *January Magazine*, October 2000, januarymagazine.com/profiles/jkrowling.html.

GENE LUEN YANG

41 "Actually, more of us feel": Joshua Barajas, "This Chinese-American Cartoonist Forces Us to Face Racist Stereotypes," *PBS News Hour*, September 30, 2016.
42 "I started being able": Ibid.
43 "I remember thinking": Christian Holub, "Gene Luen Yang Remembers 'American Born Chinese' Tenth Anniversary," *Entertainment Weekly*, September 6, 2016.
44 "Story is about tension": Julie Bartel, "One Thing Leads to Another: An Interview with Gene Luen Yang," *The Hub*, YALSA, August 28, 2014.
   "Words and images": Ibid.

BEATRIX POTTER

47 "My Dear Noel": Mackey, *Beatrix Potter's Peter Rabbit*, p. 36.
49 "I have just made": Ibid., p. 133.

C. S. LEWIS

52 "I am a product of long corridors": Lewis, *Surprised by Joy*, p. 10.
53 "Friendship is the greatest": C. S. Lewis, Letter to Arthur Greeves on December 29, 1935.
    They Stand Together: The Letters of C. S. Lewis to Arthur Greeves (1914-1963).
    Edited by Walter Hooper. New York: Macmillan, 1979, p. 477.
54 "When you give up": Lewis, *Collected Letters*, vol. 3, p. 1108-9

MADELEINE L'ENGLE

56 "I've been a writer": Tribute.ca, "Madeleine L'Engle True Story," www.tribute.ca/
    inspiration/madeleine-lengle-/144/121976, accessed December 4, 2017.
58 "We drove through": Andrew Liptak, "Madeleine L'Engle's *A Wrinkle in Time*," *Kirkus
    Reviews*, September 25, 2014, www.kirkusreviews.com/features/madeleine-
    lengles-i-wrinkle-timei.
59 "I avoided science in school": Scholastic, "Madeleine L'Engle Interview Transcript,"
    www.scholastic.com/teachers/articles/teaching-content/madeleine-lengle-
    interview-transcript, accessed December 4, 2017.
   "Isn't everything?": Cynthia Zarin, "The Storyteller: Fact, Fiction, and the Books of
    Madeleine L'Engle," *The New Yorker*, April 12, 2004.

BIBLIOGRAPHY

Angelou, Maya. *I Know Why the Caged Bird Sings*. Reissue edition. New York: Ballantine Books, 2009.

Cisneros, Sandra. *A House of My Own*. Reprint edition. New York: Vintage Books, 2016.

Cooling, Wendy. *D Is for Dahl*. New York: Viking, 2005.

Dahl, Roald. *Boy: Tales of Childhood*. New York: Puffin Books, 2013. Kindle edition.

Dean, Tanya. *Who Wrote That? Theodor Geisel (Dr. Seuss)*. Philadelphia: Chelsea House Publishers, 2002.

Fleischman, Sid. *The Trouble Begins at Eight: A Life of Mark Twain in the Wild, Wild West*. New York: HarperCollins, 2008.

Handy, Bruce. *Wild Things: The Joy of Reading Children's Literature as an Adult*. New York: Simon and Schuster, 2017.

Hurtig, Jennifer. *My Favorite Writer: Beatrix Potter*. New York: Weigl Publishers, 2009.

Johnson, Frank. *The Very Best of Maya Angelou: The Voice of Inspiration*. CreateSpace Independent Publishing Platform, 2014. Kindle edition.

Klimo, Kate. *Dr. Seuss, The Great Doodler*. New York: Random House, 2016.

Kolb, Harold H., Jr. *Mark Twain: The Gift of Humor*. Lanham, MD: University Press of America, 2014.

Lear, Linda. *Beatrix Potter: A Life in Nature*. New York: St. Martin's Press, 2007.

Lewis, C. S., *The Collected Letters of C. S. Lewis*. Vol. 2, Books, Broadcasts, and the War, 1931-1949. San Francisco: HarperOne, 2005.

Lewis, C. S. *The Collected Letters of C. S. Lewis*. Vol. 3, Narnia, Cambridge, and Joy, 1950-1963. San Francisco: HarperOne, 2007.

Lewis, C. S. *Letters to Children*. Edited by Lyle W. Dorset and Marjorie Lamp Mead. New York: Scribner, 1996.

Lewis, C. S. *Surprised by Joy: The Shape of My Early Life*. New York: Harcourt, Brace, Jovanovich, 1966.

Mackey, Margaret. *Beatrix Potter's Peter Rabbit: A Children's Classic at 100*. Lanham, MD: Scarecrow Press, 2002.

Nel, Phillip. *The Annotated Cat: Under the Hats of Seuss and His Cats*. Annotated edition. New York: Random House Books for Young Readers, 2007.

Phelps, William L. *Autobiography, with Letters*. Oxford: Oxford University Press; 7th print edition, 1939.

Smith, Sean. *J. K. Rowling: A Biography*. London: Michael O'Mara Books, 2003.

Solomon, Tom. *Roald Dahl's Marvellous Medicine*. Oxford: Oxford University Press, 2017.

Twain, Mark. *Autobiography of Mark Twain*. Vols. 1-3. Oakland: University of California Press; 2012.

Warrick, Karen Clemens. *Sandra Cisneros: Inspiring Latina Author*. New York: Enslow Pub Inc., 2009.